COMING THROUGH

For Carol
with blessings & admiration —

Renie

ALSO BY RENNIE McQUILKIN

An Astonishment and an Hissing
North Northeast
We All Fall Down
Counting to Christmas
Learning the Angels
Passage
Getting Religion
Private Collection
First & Last
The Weathering: New & Selected Poems
Visitations
Going On
A Quorum of Saints
Dogs
North of Eden: New & Collected Poems
Afterword
The Readiness
Seabury Seasons

COMING THROUGH

A BOOK OF DAYS

Poems by

Rennie McQuilkin

Antrim House
Bloomfield Connecticut

Library of Congress Control Number: 2020942311

ISBN: 978-1-943826-72-8

First Edition, 2020

Printed & bound by Book Baby, Inc,

Book design by Rennie McQuilkin

Front cover photograph: "Skunk Cabbage in Ice"
by Ian Clark

Inner title page: "Skunk Cabbage in Early Spring"
(detail, black & white) by Sara C. Foster

Author photograph by Hunter Neal, Jr.

Antrim House
860.217.0023
AntrimHouseBooks@gmail.com
www.AntrimHouseBooks.com
400 Seabury Dr., #5196, Bloomfield, CT 06002

For the dedicated caregivers at Seabury

Acknowledgments

My thanks to the editors of the following publications in which these poems first appeared in earlier versions:

The Connecticut River Review: "Matins" as ("Baptism")
Voices: "The Dancing"

I am grateful to early readers of the poems in this book, in partcular my wife, Sarah, and Katharine Carle. They have offered very helpful suggestions. I would also like to thank Ian Clark for the photograph of skunk cabage appearing on the book's front cover, as well as Sara Foster for her painting of skunk cabbage appearing on the inner title page as a black & white detail from the painting.

TABLE OF CONTENTS

PREFACE

In this Book of Days, I pick up where I left off at the end of July, 2019 in my previous book, *Seabury Seasons*. The first half of this new book reflects a relatively stable period preceding the coming of the current pandemic. Since then, the world we live in has become more and more apocalyptic. The poems in the second half of the book reflect that world, with occasional retreats to catch their breath. They look for ways to prevail against political, climactic, medical, and racial disaster. I hope you will join me in my search for a roadmap to a future made brighter by what we have learned from facing the heart of darkness.

Rennie McQuilkin
Bloomfield, CT
July 21, 2020

I always get to where I'm going
by walking away from where I've been.

Winnie the Pooh

COMING THROUGH

Knuckling Down

By the age of 10, my father
was a big time *mibster*.
Knuckled down in San José,
he flicked marbles, glass *mibs,*
with the trigger of his thumb
in the teens before the War,
played for keeps, pocketed
his neighbors' *dead ducks*
knocked out of the ring –
what beauties, those marbles
taken prisoner by his *shooters* –
aggies and *alleys* and *sulphides*
of all stripes and colors,
bumblebees, jaspers, onionskins,
greens, blues, reds, yellows . . .
swirling through them.

In these degenerate times, those
beauties of his have come out
of their mason jar and tobacco box.
Dear Father, I think you'll like
how your treasure is helping
a different sort of dead duck
or one about to be. I'm depositing
the marbles in a bowl, a ring
of them in water for desperate bees
lovely as the marbles
to cling onto with knuckled limbs
as they drink, to avoid drowning,
holding on to a life we have made
barely tenable with chemical warfare.

Thank you, Father, for the wherewithal
to help me hope we're not too late,
much as I fear
you were better at your game than I at
my long shot, though I too play for keeps.

8.3.19

Finding Elysium

A land-roving ferry took us, six old-timers,
on undulant dirt and corduroy tributaries
through Seabury's woodlands and meadows
we could no longer navigate on old shanks.

One of us referred to our driver and guide
as Charon. We laughed, a little ruefully,
but reveled in banks of asters, goldenrod,
Queen Anne's lace, verbena, Jo Pye weed . . .

and dropped down to a place called The Glen,
so secluded and peaceful a spot with its full
shading silver maple and bench for settling
that someone said, "I could stay here forever."

For a long moment, before we jolted forward,
a Monarch landed on loosestrife and drank,
wings trembling, with no thought
of further flight. Such sweetness was sufficient.

8.10.19

Protest

As town officials bandy words about
the illness sickening the body politic,
a small, umber, pig-tailed child
is working a paint roller on a handle
many times her height,
wiping out "Muslims Go Home."
At home in her work she looks straight
in the eye of the curse disappearing
beneath a field of nonjudgmental sky.
Between the cinder blocks she paints,
the spaces could be rungs on a ladder
let down from above.

8.11.19

UFOs

I'm waiting for visitations
from the emerald, cleric-collared
ruby-throateds. It's not to be.

But look –
unidentified objects are moving
too quickly to decipher, up & down
among the thick leafage of the tree
near which the hummingbird feeder
is fastened to my window.

I am being looked into by suspicious
aliens from the avian world
able to maneuver everywhichway.
It occurs to me that they may want
less humanity.

I remove impedimenta from the sill
this side of the feeder.
Now they come. How beautifully.
They have me wondering: who's alien,
who's not?

8.14.19

Orchid

for Hedy Korst

All winter it languished in the greenhouse,
leaves drooping, roots coiled like dead snakes
in the bottom of its clay pot.

Hedy said to have fairh. We had none.
What did we know of the wild white wimples
that orchid had in mind. How they soar now

like the angelic wings of "Butterfly Nuns"
in extravagant habits. It's enough to give us
religion – faith in lame limbs, dead roots.

8.17.19

Tree Smarts

for Jeff Dugan

How do trees do it?
One is leaning over Goodrich Rd.
at a 45 degree angle.
It has been doing this for eighty years.

My friend, who collects downed cedars
and anoints them with oils rubbed
into their skin, making them sculpture,
says trees are brainier than we think –

says they have architectural skills,
may tilt dangerously but still
stand, thanks to the girding they install
as a way of postponing their demise.

My friend has learned from trees –
like any Redwood riven by lightning,
he is all the stronger for his joinings.
His own anointing will have to wait.

I too lean toward earth but have found
good teachers overhead.

2.3.19 / 9.7.19

Migration

They'll be going soon, now it's fall.
Charlie too is gone, though his
courtyard's full of late blossoming
so much of which he plotted:
scant consolation, like knowing
the ruby-throated nectar-seekers,
also gone, are south of here at speeds
I can't follow – like Charlie's.

That's all prelude to this shock
of seeing two larger-than-I-remember
pairs of wings, red-orange,
yellow-and-white spotted with umber
dividers like leading in stained glass,
opening and shutting in the jubilation
of the juice of a purple butterfly bush –
so entirely here it's hard to imagine
they will winter in Mexico.

As a boy I chased such Monarchs for miles
and mounted them on cotton batting.
I mean to hold on less tightly now,
leave space in the netting for beauty to
go its own way.

9.9.19

Earth Dirt, Moon Dust

The poet says think dirt, think stone, and green
and blue like the agate of the planet. I want to.
But will the spirit be willing? Leaving the reading
I stumble, cane poking like a blind man's across
the macadam toward my awaiting guzzler, undone
by my failure to *see, oh see,* as the poet entreated us.

What I see is nothing more than a batch of weed . . .
but look – it's breaking through pavement
quite prodigiously, Mother Earth's fur.
And now from the exit ramp outside Real Art Ways
a lively crone points heavenward and good lord

I see, fully gibbous, all that moonstone
and moondust with pure liquefaction at the poles,
reminding that life persists despite time's ravaging
and the inch or two a year the moon's moving away.
I wave at her and the crone and the wily weeds,

9.11.19

Red Roses

for Kelveta Whittaker

Today the traditional stand-alone rose
sadly announces the departure of a friend
in the community where we pass the time
of our later years. But this – it's not right:

the rose in its tall narrow vase
is straggly, short, more beige than red.

I say as much to a woman blessed with color
more vibrant than mine, a joyful caregiver.
On my return three red roses rise in praise.
At times like this, color matters.

9.19.19

The Healing

after Luke 17:11-19

The place might have been a white-collar suburb
near the Alamo, through which a suspicious
mestizo was passing, to the dismay of residents,
on his way to the Church of the Holy Redeemer.
That he was disfigured and talking to himself
in a foreign tongue made matters worse.
The police were called in . . .

In fact, however, the place was a border town
between Samaria and Galilee,
and the man, a despised Samaritan and leper,
was calling out "Unclean, Unclean," a warning
as he headed toward a revival service.
Bystanders moved as far from him as possible
The man, who was white with leprosy, joined
a queue before a small figure in a white tunic.

As the healer laid hands on the other lepers,
their complexions went from ghostly white
to ruddy with hope, and it seemed a miracle
had indeed occurred. The lepers went dancing,
thankless, into the field beyond the revival tent.

When the Samaritan, last in line, approached,
the crowd cried out "No, no, don't touch him!
He is not one of us." They were supported by
two officers of the rabbi, toughs who believed in
Jewish Supremacy and tried to drag the Samaritan
from the healer. The Samaritan fell

to the feet of the Healer, who fended off the toughs
and sent them packing back to the local rabbi
before laying his hands on the man's forehead . . .

Meanwhile, back near the Alamo, the local police
are beating the mestizo, mouthing
Supremacist slogans, their bodycams turned off.

And in the Holy Land, against a sullen sky,
the Healer bends down, raises
the Samaritan to his feet and kisses his forehead:
"Your faith has made you well."

The crowd's *No's* have turned to silence.
"May it always be thus," the Healer whispers to
those closest to him. He looks to the sky.

10.14.19

Another Extinction

Woe for the loss of cursive handwriting,
all that attention to the Palmer Method
and a "good hand,"

the teacher patrolling the aisles to be sure
we wrote with our wrists, not our fingers,
fillling lined pages with elegant lettering.

The worst of losing script (more than
mailmen unable to read my addresses)
is the loss of all the creatures incarnate

in it – that plump Egyptian grouse
in the "*a*"; the heads-up cobra advancing
in "*J*"; the owl eye in "*o*"; waves in "*m*" . . .

May the natural history alive in script
come back to life. May the sweet-
flowing cursive take root in the young.
May they have a good hand in the future.

10.25.19

All Saints' Day

All-Hallows night the wind blew fiercely,
swept clean the remains of the year
from the birch, so many yellow leaves
swirling down to the underworld.

This morning of All Saints
spring's pollinating catkins are purely
clear against a sky the blue of Mary's robe,
their three-pointed promise a reminder.

11.1.19

News

Please forgo the news –
nothing new. Praise dawn,
lift your cup, toast the day.

Here's what's fit to print:
the pigeons are celebrating
last night's freeze. Look,

they're walking on water,
a thin skim of ice edging
the koi pond. *This is new!*

they seem to say, and flutter
their wings, creating a fine
many-colored spray.

11.9.19

Good Men

for Betsy and Ursula

How husbands, long dead, live on
in this place where wives so often
survive them. Memorials rise up
outside doorways. In one of them,

happily home in an umbrella stand,
a man's canes and walking sticks
with straight and rounded grips
of all sorts – ivory, bronze, wood –

cozy up to his wife's yard sticks
that once measured spurts of children
and the appointments of home,
charting its harmonious dimensions.

In another nook, two gourds,
long-necked, are posed as courting
cranes, she with her head coyly turned
aside, his thrust lovingly toward her.

11.9.19

In the End

En ma Fin gît mon Commencement:
In my end is my beginning.
                    – Mary, Queen of Scots

From my eyrie over the disappearing
koi pond, I see dusk trail lavender clouds,
not so all day, gray with threat of snow.

As the mackerel sky goes pink to purple,
the night comes on, will freeze the pond,
kill this and that, but I have seen.

11.12.19

Dessert Table

My oncologist says I am at Stage Four
and assures me that my current treatment
will work for only so long. The cancer
has an agenda and will have its way.

What my oncologist doesn't know
is that my current stage is the dessert table
in the First Congregational Church's
Saturday food pantry.

I'm the guy handing out the good stuff,
the cake and pie, Danish and brownies,
all that comes after the chow-down.
The world has gone all to hell,

but where I am is the joy that passeth
understanding of rogue cells, bill collection,
utilities turned off, and for many here,
defending a safe doorway out of the wind.

Our eyes meet close over the sweets
I hand out, and now I have for this child
a favor that comes with party cake
from a local bakery –

a glittering space traveler's ring to take her
anywhere she wants to go. She puts it on
and smiles so hugely it takes me anywhere
but where the oncologist thinks I am.

11.16.19

Endurance

Beside me, Mother was deep in *Endurance*,
Shackleton and his men stranded on ice floes,
when I began to feel an animal insistence –
though it was late at night – to go

to my stranded father, who'd lost his and our
names. At his bedside, I held his cold hand
and waited for his breaths. It seemed forever
between them, but slowly they continued,

more slowly as time went on. Then I waited
too long, too long before I heard another,
deeper, different, and after that a silent space
too empty, too vast . . .

The light was still on when I returned to Mother.
Her head was lowered, her book on the floor,
foundered. She seemed to know, said nothing,
shuddered like Shackleton's ship going under.

Next day she read to me from *Endurance* –
how after the boat went down, the crew
manned salvaged lifeboats, pushed past the ice,
reached Elephant Island, came through . . .

11.22.19

Getting Religion

Luke 19: 1-9

When Jesus is about to enter Jericho, says Luke,
(food-sellers everywhere, dealers in ikons barking
their wares, pickpockets picking, the stench . . .),

the crowd builds to such a size that Zacchaeus,
a small man, can't see to satisfy his curiosity.
So – lithe as a monkey he scales a sycamore tree

and dangles feet-first from an overhanging branch.
When Jesus passes below, he looks up quizzically,
bows deeply and blows a kiss, which so reduces
Zacchaeus to laughter that Jesus too begins to laugh,

then asks Zacchaeus to climb down and join him.
They walk side by side, and Jesus invites himself to
dinner with his new friend. That's all it takes for
Zacchaeus, the corrupt tax collector, to resolve

to return any ill-gotten kickbacks and give the poor
half his worldly possessions. The story is so zany
I believe it. I hear the laughter at dinner,
the toasts, and feel the bear hug of Jesus as he leaves.

11.24.19

Thanks Giving

for Julie and Sarah

We two old men give thanks
for the wives and nurses
who happily keep us going.

What messes they clean up
and how brilliantly they cheer
us out of our old man moaning.

This Thanksgiving we revel,
one of us flush from transfusion,
the other's blood count rising.

We too rise
to the occasion,
do a little dance, a shuffling

from chair to table
for the feasting which is
the least of our thanks giving.

11.28.19 (Thanksgiving)

Snow

Once, "snow" filled our TV screens,
(the ones with rabbit ears for amplification)
when a station signed off for the night
after the ceremonial national anthem –
a signal from the original explosion
of the universe (the particular one we're in).

When I learned what it was, I stared into it,
wondering how many of my own atoms
were formed on that occasion when the speed
of light was nothing compared to the speed
with which Something came of Nothing,
to which I returned at a speed that dizzied me,
too fast to see any angels en route.

11.28.19

The Crossing

Oh, oh was all I could say, my breath stopped
as caravans of cars to the north and south
stopped, headlights on in the grey gloaming
while a moose gangled back and forth
like a crossing guard,
head up as if to say to the cars "Stay back,
let him cross." The small calf, wobbling
on the far side of the road, advanced and fell
back, unsure its mother's repeated crossings
promised safe passage.

Finally, the moose, shaking her head,
moved toward the nearest car
as if to charge it, then returned to the calf
and once more cleared the way, like a tackle
blocking for the runner, which the calf now
became, racing across the divide and into
underbrush on the other side. The cars,
blinking lights, sounded like New Year's Eve.

12.4.19

Praise Song

*The nocturnal African dung beetle is the only
known non-vertebrate to navigate and orient
itself by the Milky Way.*

Now let us praise Dung Beetles who
roll balls of excrement towering
over them. Faced with such an ordeal,
Sisyphus might have called it quits.
But these leggy, body-armored fellows
sculpt, roll, and stash away fecal stuff
250 times their own weight nightly
for progeny born in the bosom of dung.

See them clamber to the top
of their globes and orient themselves
by the stars, dead-reckoning
like ancient Polynesians
at home in their wilderness of ocean.

12.13.19

For the Child Disturbing the Peace at St. John's

"Get that child out of here," one parishioner hissed
when a child persisted in hammering his pew.
Others, more discreet, issued shushings *sotto voce*

as the candlelight service of Lessons & Carols broke
into a carol in which the three Wise Men hammer
at the door of the inn where there is no room.

I smiled at the congruity of the child, and recalled
a Posada procession in Cuernavaca in which children,
singing *Ora Pro Nobis*, went from house to house,

knocking on the doors they passed, turned away by all
until one opened to them, a crèche
in its courtyard and a piñata holding gifts of candy.

I imagined the Christ Child knocking his manger slats
with swaddled feet, anxious to feed. Praised be the child,
the trouble-maker. He knocks at the door of my heart.

12.15.19

Children's Pageant

The angel announcing the Good News
(a 6-year-old with huge pasteboard wings)
must have been hiding behind the pulpit.
When she rose up huge, she staggered us
no less than the five crook-staffed boys
tending white-sheeted, fur-capped sheep.

It all went according to schedule under
a shining tinfoil star on a ten-foot pole.
Three camels (each with four denim legs)
mounted the stage from the nave,
led by crowned, red-robed 8th graders;
and tarp-covered oxen followed suit.

When time came for "The First Noel,"
the cast around the congregational crèche
signed the carol with hands and paws
for the deaf lady in the first pew.
Even the small Christ Child joined in.

12.22.19

At the Callanish Stones

on the Isle of Lewis in the Outer Hebrides, 2001

Rugged, uncivilized giants, these monoliths
in the late-night gloaming this far north
circle eccentrically, stone silent, waiting for
solstice and sacrifice, listening
to the "extinct" corncrake still at it, rasping
like a rough file, and to the ghostly skirling
of a bagpiper in the brume of the valley below.
So much will not say no.

12.29.19

Matins

I've become unglued, the magnet holding
my name tag to me having flown the coop
when I threw off my daily duds too fast
last night. This is all too apt.

How I am dying, let me not count the ways
but sip a half-hazelnut, half-dark-roast brew
at the window overlooking the koi pond
unfrozen in this January thaw, take delight

in a mauve and pink pigeon descending,
no white dove, just a pigeon off the streets
taking the waters, happily dipping its beak.

1.12.20

The Dancing

We mean to enjoy our new lives is the motif
of these panelists diagnosed with Alzheimer's.
One speaks of black holes in his brain scan
but there's laughter and joy in all they say.
In the Q&A, one of the panelists, my friend,
stumbles down the auditorium aisle,
calling my name loudly enough for all to hear.
He throws his arms around me, kisses me,
says "My id's on the loose." He swings me
as his dancing partner, says I am one thing
he hasn't forgotten, holds me at arm's length,
recalls a poem I sent him about my father
growing gentle and loving in his dementia.
Then back to our dance, uncivilized dance of
two bears, civil as never before, he with gaps
in his brain, I with feet and legs gone numb,
chest excavated to dig out its cancer.
"We are a pair, all right," I say. And he laughs
his larger-than-life laugh. On we go, dancing
and dancing . . .

1.16.20

Incident

for Betsy and Shirley

Today a group of us meet by the *cubbies*
where we stay in touch with each other.
We surround two of our kind in trouble,
one who has lost her walker and another
just back from hospital, her brain having
cut its connection to her feet – stopped
midstride. We gather about them like cells
rushing to the site of an injury, called up
to defend our kind, keep them moving on.

1.28.20

Elegy with Apology

for Carter Elwood (1936-2019)

Your daughter (I'd forgotten you had one)
has written to say you never recovered
from a fall a few months before you went under.

We were close sixty years ago, cycled together
through Scandinavia, held onto the backs
of trucks lumbering up steep Norwegian hills,

let loose downhill, bent for speed.
You said we'd best stay together in case of flats
or whatever else might befall us. But something

in me pulled away. One day I raced off alone.
When we met at our hostel that night, you railed
and I railed back. A crack opened between us

and widened. It would never be the same.
In the years that followed, we drifted apart,
I into poetry, you into Russian Studies. We wrote

seldom, only at holidays, and then formally.
But if all time is now, we are still laughing uphill
behind diesels, downhilling wildly, never falling.

And what if I had stopped that day, a mile ahead,
waited for you to catch up, and gone on amicably
into Finland? I would start over there.

1.30.20

Groundhog Sunday

I am departing for Sunday service,
today's theme the Presentation of
Baby Jesus in the Temple – sweet

relief from our latter-day Herod's
Massacre of the Innocents and
too much more

suggested by the dark shadow
cast by our local groundhog
(oh endless winter). Now *this:*

the gate of the parking garage
is stuck half way up, too low to let
air out of my tires and sneak under.

I call Security, and a badged man
takes the heavy gate-chain in hand
and slowly, painfully,

raises the door. It rises, link by link,
and I am reminded God's child
came, they say, to raise Heaven's

gate. I thank the young man in white
from Security, who smiles so benignly
I remember divinity is always nigh.

2.2.2020

Daughter

See him shoveling a path to the barn
through two feet of snow,
making his way up a 30-foot ladder
to the hay mow, and from there
up another ladder to the cupola.

He opens a sash unused for years,
leans out to place on the sill
what he has carried, bundled carefully
as the child his wife is holding close –
the three Roman Candles

that will send the promised signal to
his neighbor in Wyckoff
to say "It's a girl!" He lights the wicks
and sends flares into the sky. If a boy,
no fireworks.

2.17.20

Matins II

May I model myself on the mourning dove
whose song, as he rises in courtship flight
this mid-February day, serenades an intended
(if only the sky) with the vibrato of a song
not from his beak but from the excitation
of his wings' whir, his whole body vibrating
with Love. So it was in the beginning.

2.17.20

Baptism, St. John's

Down the center aisle of St. John's
the rector processes after baptism.
She carries the cross-marked child
on high before her like a figurehead
on the prow of a ship, his face shining
with the water of salvation still on it,
just as she often holds the Bible aloft
to praise it at the heart of the nave.
May Time, gnawing today's imprint
on this child, not entirely erase it.

2.18.20

Found

The cane I stranded in a grocery cart at the market
had a figured sheen like a newly molted milk snake.
Its staff sparkled as it balanced me.

I was bereft, until Rita called to say she'd found it
and wanted to return it, except her car wouldn't start
and her feet were bad (spent the day before in ER).

Her voice quavered and she couldn't control a stutter.
When I found it in me to say she should keep the cane
she said "Oh-oh-oh, do-do you mean-mean-mean it?"

The cane and I are now more found than ever.
Though neither Rita nor I can get to Sunday service
it hardly seems to matter.

2.23.20

The Lark Ascending

Hail to thee, blithe Spirit!
Bird thou never wert,
That from Heaven, or near it,
Pourest thy full heart ...
                            Shelley

Amid pestilence, rising seas, shrinking species,
Vaughn Williams' Lark Ascending is faint,
but now I listen harder, abandon the Times,

travel to East Anglia, 1952, the heath –
a morning dreary as this, when out of a tangle
of gorse and underbrush, Shelley's blithe Spirit

turns from verse to a wild spiraling thing rising
out of sight and singing all the more purely
for its invisibility –

May I live at will in a time as present as this.

2.26.2

Plague

Stark, this first Sunday in Lent 2020
starting with news the Virus is spreading
medievally – too like the other Plague.
A home for elders like my own is a target.

At church today, 700 years disappear.
Stark, the choir circling the nave
thrice, silent but for its soft *Lord deliver us,*

the Crucifix going before it for protection
like the arms I cross across my chest
at the rail, fearing infection in the wafer
and the wine, though it is a strong Port,

the Rector says – proof against the Virus.
If that weren't so funny . . . Trust Mondavi
to protect us?

Are the ashes still smudged on our heads kin
to the *ashes ashes* of the chant from those dire
days of yore telling us *we all fall down?*
We pray to rise from this occasion.

3.1.20

Orchestration in a Time of Plague

All night the birch at my window
was windy, sometimes drumming me
awake, sometimes swishing branches
like the brushings of a snare drum,
sometimes simply singing
with the tips of its twigs, delighting
me back to sleep.

These days when friends must keep
their distance, it's good to have one
that near, even one so moody.

3.2.20

Tea in a Time of Plague

The glacier knocks in the cupboard
The desert sighs in the bed,
And the crack in the tea-cup opens
A lane to the land of the dead.

W. H. Auden

In the hall I hear the clock counting
on the ravaging of Time, whose ally,
Covid, camps close by,
biding, invisible in its camouflage,

its scouts already in, loosening locks,
knowing victory is a matter of time.
Meanwhile it's time for tea. I look
at leaves in the bottom of the cup,

see a hairline crack in the bone china,
think of Auden's Staffordshire service
rattling, the poet following a crack
in his cup to Underworld circles,

his face reflecting in amber
like mine as I trace a line of thought
to my mother, teetering on the brink
during the Spanish Flu pandemic.

She was ten and I minus eighteen
close to not becoming – then
the miracle. Now I listen for scouts
within. Are two miracles too much?

3.17.20

Birdwalk

Oh verse beyond my means these days –
the *cheerily cheerily* of a robin,
the *I am here* of a wood thrush,
the *It's so good* of a goldfinch,
and the whistle Sarah whistled at a cat bird,
waiting while that high-tailed comedian
paused to think it over, then plagiarized.

3.24.20

Visiting the Star Magnolia

On twin canes, four-footed as a Hopi deer dancer,
in sedate procession over hieroglyphic tar marks
in the gloaming of the day, I complete my ritual
journey to a Star Magnolia, where my spirits are
raised before its ten-petaled blossoms, out just today.
Bent over before the tree, I revel among its gold-
centered white stars.

3.27.29

God's Work

When the Plague struck Spain in 1347,
the Christian spree of killing Jews, Moors,
anyone not a true Believer
had to be suspended,
giving the Moors of Granada time
to build the Alhambra, Hanging Gardens,
all the wonders Christians claimed
when the Plague abated
sufficiently for Ferdinand and Isabella
to return to the killing, start the Inquisition
and all the horrors we call civilization.
Too bad we never took History 101.

3.31.20

Dogs in a Time of Plague

In Brooklyn, Queens, Trieste, everywhere
in cities across the globe, sirens wail.
All day the dogs howl.

At night the dogs come close,
burrow in bed with us.
We murmur to them, they murmur back.

3.28.20

Essential Work

is what, in the midst of plague,
a woodsman does, bending
down to smell the essence
of a tiny marsh marigold's
minute and gilded goings-on.

4.4.20 (for Ian Clark)

Coming Out

Today for the first time I am hiding
my mouth and nose beneath the white
of a medical mask, barely recognize
myself when I look in the glass,
wonder who I will be when the virus
is over and we all come out of hiding.
Will we be redone as caterpillars are
within hard cases of chrysali, emerging
winged, no longer devouring the world?

4.6.20

Earth Day

On porches surrounding a courtyard
full of spring flowers endangered by
a cold spell, in their midst a pondful
of koi (small reds and whites, not fed
since fall, barely breathing),

our hands freeze in sudden flurries.
We are gripping song sheets, singing
to each other, daring the Pestilence –
we few intent on beating the odds.

4.22.20

"Raindrop Prelude"

for Frédéric Chopin and George Sand

His études, preludes, nocturnes
having played beside me all night,
I wake to the sound of doves
close by my window: courtship
wing-whistlings, cooings refuting
the *nevermores* of a raven.

Escaping a pandemic raging like
the inflammation of tuberculosis
in Frédéric, I am transported
to Mallorca that winter of 1837
when he and his hot-headed love
pursue their arts, high up
in the monastery at Valldemossa.

One cold, rainy morning she wakes
to a kreeing of eagles close above,
reminding her how shunned she
and her Chopin are on this Eden
of an island, their unwed state
a disgrace, not to mention her
cross-dressing, her cigars . . .

Miserable as she is, George feels
something other than her usual
fury. Behind her, Frédéric plays
a piece he has worked on all night,
coughing steadily but persisting.
In a mirror he sees her knotted face

relent, inhabit the music, radiate
a joy that will outlive

distresses to come: sickness, decline,
dissension, the death of more
than Chopin – a world gone wrong.

5.5.20

Hummingbird

The latest plague is lively, spores of infection
rolling about down in the courtyard below
like pinballs at a penny arcade
searching for an opening to drop in.

I am waiting for a ruby-throated hummingbird
to appear at the flowered feeder attached
to my window. I am sitting by a white orchid
on a heart-shaped trellis in its pot, the last

of eight from Saint Valentine's Day,
two of its petals folded demurely like wings
about its hidden parts. I am nursing it
with small sips of water.

Outside, white spores float by, cottonwood seed
looking for a place to lodge? Across the way
two of my friends are sick with the Pestilence,

their window closed. An "air-scrubber" is at work,
cleansing their world. Near them, a white-haired
elder, bright as a bird, opens a window.
At her distance, she seems to float above the globe

of my feeder. The woman is cleaning her window.
It shines. Next to her a sign reads *BLESS*.
I half expect her to dart into the sky.

5.19.20

The Circling

for Bill and Bob

I am weightless these Days of Plague,
rising up and circling like a woodcock
over friends breathing hard in ICUs.
I am in love with whoever
is stricken, piping my song as I make
my rounds in an air more dire and dear
than ever before. I will not return
to earth, spiraling down in joy,
until my friends breathe clearly again.

5.21.20

Evensong in a Time of Plague

Atop the thick, square-topped cedar posts
of a fence separating Pestilence from
a singing, trilling, wind-woven meadow,

walkers untouched by the plague have placed
umber, white, gray, red, black and ivory stones,
some shaped like birds, some set with eyes,

some with the profiles of humankind . . .
In the gloaming, as the chapel carillon chimes,
the stones, in memory of those who have fallen,

seem faces of a world-wide choir, their robes
the posts below. They lift voices with those
in the meadow, promising perfect health.

5.21.20

For a Naval Man Safely Home

for Bob and Nan Skeele

I am placing a stone for you, my friend,
on one of the posts along the waving sea
of a meadow full of song and livelihood.

Your stone bears the swells on which
you made your way
to port. Centered on it is an anchor,

sign you will always rest in the haven
of the heart of the woman who held you
when you arrived at your destination.

5.25.20 (Memorial Day)

Elegy for a Barn Man

for Lowell

How exposed to the world
we feel without you, Lowell,
whose aperture was always
perfect for the hay-filled bays
you led us to. Such barns!

You will live
forever in a fine one now,
one of those *many mansions*.
Please reserve more bays
near yours for us.

5.29.20

The Coloring

It was the hottest news at Allendale School:
George Mahoney, the janitor/handiman
was going with Janet O'Malley,

he leanly Irish, she blowsy, big-breasted.
server of tasty sweets in the kitchen.
That was 70 years ago, but still sizzles,

as does the summer I worked with George
painting the school redder and redder.
He showed me how not to stint on paint,

keep the brush loaded and sloshing back
and forth, like a cow's tongue on a block
of salt, said George, a farm boy from Cork.

All the while, I saw him savoring salty
Janet. I smiled my way through that job.
I try not to think, but can't stop thinking

of the way Allendale went up in flames,
for the insurance, skeptics claimed –
all that joy turned to smoke.

But still I see George grin as he said
I might have a future in painting. This
coloring is for you, George. I am your man.

6.1.20

My Mother's Wreath

I've wired my mother's fruited wreath
to the front door after it fell with a terrible
clanging of its bells like the fire engines
she knew as a girl. Not meant for disaster,

those small copper bells
hanging from varicolored streamers are
dead ringers for the ones that chimed
on the horse-drawn sleigh she loved.

I couldn't bear to see the wreath lie
crumpled like her during the Spanish Flu.
Wiring it to the door I might have been
wiring her

together again like a broken marionette.
I worked the wreath this way and that
to hang it precisely as it had hung. Now,
when I open the door, it's her.

6.8.20

Stitchings

The *Darning Needles,* those bright,
iridescent dragonflies, are unaware
of the Pestilence. But in my state
of distraction, their dartings seem
to patch the sick air,

calling up another stitching in '43
when the campers at Camp Overalls
knitted for the boys abroad: wool caps,
covers for bare toes protruding from
casts, shields for amputated stumps . . .

We knitted faster and faster, not to
think too much, just as good people
now are quickly stitching masks
to fight an infiltrating enemy. We won
the other war, will win this one.

6.9.20

Distancing

I suppose mystery is good for me
but how much? Under this sky full
of fireflies, I wonder
if they always light up as they fly
and how with such small wings they fly

so fast, and what it is like for a body
to light up so entirely – not just itself
but everything around it.
(Once, when one got into my bedroom
that small a thing lit the whole room.)

I am distracted from my wondering by
a cricket, wanting to know how it feels
to scrape one leg (upper or lower?) over
the jagged teeth of the other leg.

So much distancing between me and them.
Couldn't I, just for a while, try out
as a firefly or a cricket? These plague-ridden
days of aloofing, I have a need
to be less distant from my fellow creatures.

6.22.20

Mockingbird at the Peak

1. Mockingbird at Dusk in a Time of Plague

May the mockingbird singing on a peak
over the stricken in Skilled Nursing
please them as it rushes from song to song
in the Blue Hour before day is done.

If only its borrowed offering could outlast
the short time before night snuffs it out
and the moon-boat, slender-hulled, sails
silently toward whatever shore awaits.

2. Mockingbird Communion

The mockingbird singing on a peak
of Skilled, rushing from song to song
in the Blue Hour before day is done
urges on the slender hull of a moon-
boat in which two survivors
of the various plagues life can offer,
looking up and out,
find themselves sailing to a place
the music of their communion creates.

6.25.20

Sacrilege

I have qualms about total obedience,
as did the prosecutors at Nuremberg
and many a bride at the altar.

Here is Abraham, obeying Jehovah,
setting forth to the place of sacrifice,
telling Isaac (like Christ) to carry
the means of his own execution –

the pile of wood and the sharp knife
that Abraham knows will be used
for the ritual slaying of his son
though he is mum about his intent.

I have difficulty with such obedience
and am not relieved of it
when Abraham desists in the end,

only because Jehovah says, *Good man,*
for obeying – now put down that knife.

6.30.20

Praise Song for Burdock

for B.J. Hardersen

The common burdock is not least among
the flowers of the field praised by
a song sparrow in its soaring three-part hymn,

and is the joy of a passer-by, remembering
how once she wove burrs and blooms of burdock
into a crown.

These plague-ridden days, she knows,
when chewed it kills germs. She stops, picks a leaf,
moves on more happily.

7.1.20

Chair Yoga in Quarantine

Tuned into Chair Yoga on Channel 918,
Seated Mountain our first position, we quarantined
elders celebrate our animal nature virtually.

We throw ourselves into the Cat & Cow Stretch,
our hands turning to claws flexing on thighs, then
lean back, stretching wide as cows ruminating,
happily multi-stomached; now make sharp beaks

of our twined hands, thrust them skyward,
roll our shoulders, extend our eagle arms, and glide
back down to earth, Seated Mountains again;
pause, breathe deeply, slide legs apart, feet together

in the butterfly position, then morph into dolphins,
fin-feet working back and forth, forth and back;
and settle into a stillness so complete we might be
leopards in tall grass, waiting . . .

Assuming position after position, too feral for Plague
to afflict, we end by wrapping our arms around
our shoulders like wings, hugging ourselves. Namaste.

7.2.20

Fireworks in Connecticut

Along the Great Tidal River called *Kwenitegok* by the First People,
from East Hartford to Windsor and beyond, barges unleash
a barrage of blossoming lights, loud, louder, loudest – an answer
to the Pestilence raging in the land.

Surely such muscling of the sky must impress the gods, erase
whatever anger they harbor. Meanwhile a full moon continues
its deliberate rise from salmon to white, climbing the sky, oblivious
to the circusing all around it.

Nothing will wipe a cratered smile off the face of the Moon.
The tree frogs go on trilling despite all the ruckus; the fireflies
pepper the meadow with their own fire works as they did
for eons before the First People named the Long Tidal River,

and will long after our human kind no longer walk the land,
having misunderstood far more than how to pronounce *Kwenitegok*.

7.4.20 (IndependenceDay)

Alarm in a Time of Plague

for Colin

Who would have thought an incinerated bagel
stuck in a toaster could make so much smoke!
Soon the sirens, red flashing lights, big engines
and a blue-blazing cruiser pulling up outside,
tall men in tall boots and tall hats clumping in,
installing an enormous fan, defogging the place . . .

After they leave, the Security guard who was first
on the crime scene, returns from the dark far below,
tendering the red-and-yellow hummingbird feeder
he'd dislodged and sent tumbling three stories
when he'd thrown open a window to save our lungs.

This morning we are luxuriating in a smoke-free place
that smells deliciously like a campfire ground
the morning after a cookout. I am filling the feeder
to bring back beauty.

7.11.20

Romance of the Pigeons

Our oasis is overrun by a mess of pigeons.
One of us clangs a pot to scatter them.
Today a she-pigeon emerges from a bush,
edges close to a chest-puffed he-pigeon
all iridescent lavender, teal, purple . . .

Courtly, he circles her, fantail sweeping,
one wing raised like a sail. Now
she lifts her beak to his. They touch beaks
again and again (tenderly I'm tempted to say,
understanding now what billing is),
after which she flattens herself, becomes
a part of the earthscape.

He rides her so briskly this doesn't seem
the point of it all. What is is all that showing
and kissing, and now this delighted preening
that follows – before they disappear
into the boudoir-bush from which she emerged.
That it's home becomes clear when he bursts
out to chase off a contender for his lady's favor.

7.12.20

Anniversary on the Porch

Celebrating two years of busy ease in Independent Living
and sixty years of marriage, happily dependent
on the love of one another,
we commemorate a 1960 wedding breakfast
by feasting on pancakes swimming in dark amber syrup,
not ready ourselves to be fossilized in amber.
We revel in the circling, fan-tailed, wing-raised courtship
dance of many-colored pigeons below our eyrie and await
a Ruby-throated at our yellow-flowered porch feeder,
an emerald and red-gorged celebrant, white-collared,
proper cleric to administer our renewal of wedding vows.

7.16.20

Dancing with God

I am swayed by the dance of the organist –
his fingers, wrists, arms, legs all going at it,
and the feet, the feet sliding heel and toe,
toe and heel from pedal to pedal.

When the Word of the Lord is abroad,
I love to watch the sign-er relaying it whole-
heartedly with every inch of her body. I too.
The Good News goes straight to my limbs.
I am a tree weaving in the Wind of God.

7.19.20

ABOUT THE AUTHOR

Rennie McQuilkin was Poet Laureate of Connecticut from 2015 through 2018. His work has appeared in *The Atlantic, Poetry, The Southern Review, The Yale Review, The Hudson Review, The American Scholar, Crazyhorse,* and elsewhere. This is his nineteenth poetry collection. He has received a number of awards for his work, including fellowships from the National Endowment for the Arts and the Connecticut Commission on the Arts, as well as a Lifetime Achievement Award from the Connecticut Center for the Book. In 2010 his volume of new and selected poems, *The Weathering,* was awarded the Center's annual poetry prize under the aegis of the Library of Congress; and in 2018, *North of Eden* received the Next Generation Indie Book Award in Poetry. For nine years he directed the Sunken Garden Poetry Festival, which he co-founded at Hill-Stead Museum in Farmington, Connecticut. With his wife, the artist Sarah McQuilkin, he lives at Seabury in Bloomfield, CT.

This book is set in Garamond Premier Pro, which had its genesis in 1988 when type-designer Robert Slimbach visited the Plantin-Moretus Museum in Antwerp, Belgium, to study its collection of Claude Garamond's metal punches and typefaces. During the fifteen hundreds, Garamond – a Parisian punch-cutter – produced a refined array of book types that combined an unprecedented degree of balance and elegance, for centuries standing as the pinnacle of beauty and practicality in type-founding. Slimbach has created a new interpretation based on Garamond's designs and on compatible italics cut by Robert Granjon, Garamond's contemporary.

Copies of *Coming Through* can be ordered
at all bookstores including Amazon
and diretly from the author at
400 Seabury Dr., Apt. 5196
Bloomfield, CT 06002.

•

For more information on the work of Rennie McQuilkin
visit www.antrimhousebooks.com/authors.html.
The author can be contacted at
RMcQuil36@gmail.com.